EVANGELISM

EVANGELISM

THE CHRISTIAN'S RESPONSIBILITY

ROGER G JOHANSEN

heritagehillspress.com

Copyright © 2021 by Roger Johansen

Published by Heritage Hills Press, LLC
   Box 562
   201 N. Race Street
   Spring Hill, Kansas 66083

All rights reserved. No part of this publication may be reproduced, stored in a retrieval system or transmitted in any form by any means, electronic, mechanical, photocopy, recording or otherwise, without the prior permission of the publisher, except as provided for by USA copyright law. Heritage Hills Press is a registered trademark in the United States of America.

First printing, 2021
Cover image by Heritage Hills Press®
Printed in the United States of America

Scripture quotations are from the *New American Standard Bible*®. Copyright © The Lockman Foundation 1960, 1962, 1963, 1968, 1971, 1972, 1973, 1975, 1977, 1995. Used by permission.

Italics in biblical quotes indicate emphasis added.

Print ISBN: 978-1-7373327-2-5
Digital ISBN: 978-1-7373327-3-2

CONTENTS

From The Author — vii

Introduction — 1

1. Prayer — 7
2. Preparation — 13
3. Proclamation — 23
4. Purpose — 32
5. Perception — 37
6. Provision — 44

7	Praise	47
8	Conclusion	50

FROM THE AUTHOR

I want to praise my Lord for saving my soul. I want to thank God for all His faithful people who prayed for me and shared God's loving truths. I thank God for Dr. Raiford, Dr. Decker, and Dr. Jimmy Stallard who encouraged me to write to the glory of God in the area of evangelism. Today, these men are in glory; not evangelizing anymore, but exalting our risen Savior. I want to thank my wife Crystal in always being a great helpmate. She is my *"lily among thorns"* (Song of Solomon 2:2).

This booklet is to aid every Christian—the pastor and the layman—in the awesome privilege of sharing the good news of Christ. It is our responsibility. There is much to be shared about this topic, and certainly more to be taught than what I have written. My point in this booklet was to give something clear, concise, and helpful as a guide for this great responsibility of ours. May God be glorified, and may the Christian evangelize!

Introduction

Acts 1:8 "...and you shall be My witnesses..."

Walter accepted Christ inside his hut under the Peruvian moonlight in the jungle foothills of the Andes Mountains. There had been a mission team working with Walter during the summer. Two of the team members spent considerable time with him, walking through all aspects of the gospel. Yet, before this, there was already a missionary who had slowly been planting seeds in Walter's life for quite some time.

So, here is an interesting question: who *led* Walter to Christ? Was it the two members of the mission team that shared the good news of Jesus that led Walter to Christ? Was it the mission team that showed Christ's sacrificial love? Was it the missionary living in Peru who planted the seeds earlier? Beyond that, was it the collective prayer of different churches praying for God to save Walter's soul? What is the right answer? What we do know is that each of these people had a part in the evangelization process of Walter.

1 Corinthians 3:8 reminds the Christian that each person in the evangelism process *"will receive his own reward."* God allowed each Christian to have the privilege to be a part of evangelizing Walter. The "who" in leading Walter to the Lord was the collective effort of each person. However, 1 Corinthians 3:7 gives the proper perspective of evangelism, making clear that it is God *"who causes the growth."* Let me be clear: salvation is a work of God from beginning to end. Jesus is the author of faith (Hebrews 12). It is God that saves.

This truth ought to encourage each Christian. It is not our responsibility to "save" sinners. What man can die as a perfect sacrifice to please the righteous demands of a Holy God? Who has the power to rise from the dead and give eternal life? Only God can save sinful man. However, God has given the responsibility of evangelism to the Christian. Without the good news of Christ being shared, no one gets saved (Romans 10:13-15).

In God's sovereign plan for this age, He wants to use man to share the good news of Christ. The animal world is not sharing the gospel. The clouds do not give sufficient revelation to share the gospel of Christ. The angels, for this age, do not have this responsibility of evangelism. God has given this great task to the Christian (Luke 24:46-47).

Does that mean that a sinner will not get saved if the Christian does not share the gospel of Christ? God is the author of salvation. He knows who will be saved (John 6:64; Ephesians 1:4-5). God wants to use the Christian in the process of saving a soul. If one fails to share, God will raise up another Christian to share the gospel. Remember, God is sovereign and saves to the uttermost (Romans 8:28-30). God took Philip from Samaria to a desert road (Acts 8:26). Why would God take Philip there? God in His sovereign power knew that Philip would share Christ (Acts 8:35), and that the Ethiopian eunuch would get saved (Acts 8:37). God will find His "Philips" to get the right message to His "Ethiopian eunuchs."

The Christian has been tasked with evangelizing. A pastor once shared that the purpose of the church is to be like Christ. As one seeks to be like Christ, there are three tasks to be done. There may be variances of these three main tasks, but they all eventually come under these three. They are the three "E"s.

The first task is to *exalt* God in all that is done. The second task is to *edify* the saints. The third task is to *evangelize* the lost. If the Christian fails to do one of these tasks, has he not failed in his purpose for being a Christian on this earth? Second Corinthians 5:10 reminds the Christian that he must appear before the judgment seat of Christ. What will Christ judge? According to 2 Corinthians 5, it will be the believer's deeds. First Corinthians 3:14-15 describes a judgment not for salvation, but for rewards.

What "deeds" should the Christian be about? It appears that it would be the "deeds" that God has purposed. If we fail to witness Christ (Acts 1:8), are we not failing to fulfill a "deed" that He has given? The great commission of Matthew 28, unfortunately for many Christians, becomes the great omission. To that Christian, the great omission results in omission of rewards at the judgement seat of Christ. So, evangelism is a great importance to God.

I have observed that most Christians want to evangelize. However, the task can be difficult. It can appear overwhelming. Sometimes the fear of man keeps one from sharing the good news of Christ. There are many obstacles to try to throw the Christian off task. One pastor has described these obstacles as "bridges" that need to be crossed.

The first bridge is the *bridge of contact*. How does one make contact with the unsaved? The second bridge is the *bridge of turning* the conversation to Christ. How does the Christian do that without feeling awkward? The last bridge is the *bridge of appeal*. How does one appeal to the unsaved to get saved? Hopefully, this little book will aid you in understanding how to cross those bridges. My hope is to encourage the church to fulfill its responsibility of evangelism. Remember, the results of evangelism are up to God. If He desires to save the whole city, He can (like Nineveh in Jonah [Luke 11:32]). The task of evangelism is the Christian's responsibility.

What does the responsibility of evangelism entail? I have discovered seven areas of responsibilities in relation to evangelism. They are prayer, preparation, proclamation, purpose, perception, provision, and praise. We will unpack each of these in the remaining chapters.

| 1 |

Prayer

Acts 2:42 "They were continually devoting themselves...to prayer."

Prayer is the lifeline of the Christian. It is the Christian communicating with God (John 17:1). This is such a powerful form of communication. We live in a world where communication is a large market. One can be in a remote corner of the world, and yet clearly hear the voice of a relative thousands of miles away. How does that happen? Think about the technology behind such powerful communication! However, believers have always had one of the greatest communication devices—prayer. The words of a humble servant, anywhere in the world, can transmit into the ears of the King of heaven. This communication does not depend on place, distance, batteries, transmitters, nor satellites. What powerful communication!

The King of Kings delights in hearing the prayers of His servants. Our prayer is an expression of faith in a Holy God of hope. My wife and I visited Hampton Court in England. The well-kept gardens were impressive. The royal rooms were filled with history and prestige. One chamber was a large hall where the nobles of the land would sit. They knew that the king would soon pass through the hall from one room to another. When the king entered the room, the nobles would bow on their knees, and hold out a written request. Each hoped that today would be the day that the king attends to their petition. As Christians, we do not have to worry if God will attend to our request. We can have confidence, as we pray according to His will, that the King of kings takes time to hear our petitions (1 John 5:14).

EVANGELISM - 9

The first responsibility of a Christian in evangelism is prayer. Prayer expresses our dependence on God to save a soul eternally. Colossians 4:2 reminds the Christian to devote oneself to prayer. The context is related to evangelism. Colossians 4:2-6 could be themed as: "The Christian needs to be persistent in his prayer and participation for evangelism." The command "devote" (Col. 4:2) has the idea of an activity in which one is continually engaged. One activity is prayer for evangelism. Notice that there is within that prayer time the need to keep alert (Col. 4:2). Why does one need to be alert? What dangers lurk around prayer? There could be the possibility of giving up faith in praying for evangelism (Luke 18:7-8). The Christian could give up hope thinking that his prayers are not helping to save that dear lost one. The Christian is to be alert. The Christian is to faithfully give thanks for God's work in saving the lost.

What should the Christian pray for in relation to evangelism? Paul asked for prayer that God would *"...open up to us a door for the word"* (Col. 4:3). I knew a lady that always seemed to be sharing her faith with someone. When I inquired more on how she gets these contacts, she shared that she starts her day by asking God to give her opportunities to share Him. She was asking for open doors to the gospel. We need to ask God to open doors so that we can share the Word of God.

We need to ask God to help us to speak of Christ in a way that is clear. Paul asked for this (Col. 4:4). If the apostle Paul asked for clarity in speech, how much more ought we ask for clarity? Paul continued to remind the believers at Colossae that their response to the lost ought to *"...be with grace, as though seasoned with salt"* (Col 4:6). A Christian is to be bold in speech (Acts 4:31), but not arrogant. Arrogance does not encourage others, but a salty gracious tongue does. Our speech ought to be with gracious, thoughtful words.

We need wisdom in dealing with the lost. Paul reminded believers that the lost needed to see godly wisdom in them when he said: *"Conduct yourselves with wisdom toward outsiders"* (Col. 4:5). Jesus said that we are to be light to this dark world (Matthew 5:14). We are to show that we are different, because of the gospel of Christ. We need to ask God for wisdom on how to evangelize different peoples. We need to be wise and evangelize.

More will be said on purposeful living for evangelism, but at this point, we need to remember to pray for wisdom on how to approach those outside the faith of Christ.

The Scriptures are clear that Christ's followers ought to pray for laborers to be sent to share the truths of Christ. Christ saw others with eyes of compassion. Matthew 9:38 encourages the believer to *"...beseech the Lord of the harvest to send out workers into His harvest."* It is said that the amount of young people getting into mission work has decreased. This may be a result of less people beseeching the Lord to send forth laborers. Do you pray for God to raise up missionaries to share Him?

Interestingly, the church at Antioch prayed before sending forth Paul and Barnabas (Acts 13:3). Not every mission field is a harvest field. However, every missionary ought to be seeking those who will put their faith in Christ (Romans 1:5). The Church of God should consistently ask the Lord in prayer to raise up more laborers to share the good news of Christ. We, as Christians, need to see the lost with eyes of compassion. Once we have eyes of compassion, we will have words of prayer for God to send helpers to a needy world.

I knew of a man that weekly evangelized. He shared Christ to numerous people. He would write down the names of those in whom God has allowed in his sphere of influence. It may have been someone in the neighborhood, family, or in the workplace. He would pray daily for each person by name. He would let the person know that he was praying for them. This led to many opportunities of sharing Christ.

How is your prayer life? The disciples observed Jesus' prayer life, and asked Him to teach them to pray (Luke 11:1). Are we too busy to pray? Think about this: are we too busy to pray for the eternal salvation of others? God has given Christians the great privilege to pray about evangelism. Somehow, in some way, the Sovereign Lord uses the prayers of His children for the work of evangelism. We have that great task. We have the responsibility to pray for evangelism.

| 2 |

Preparation

1 Peter 3:15 "But sanctify Christ as Lord in your hearts, always being ready to make a defense to everyone who asks you to give an account for the hope that is in you, yet with gentleness and reverence."

Another responsibility for the Christian in relation to evangelism is *preparation*. It is said, "If you want to teach a parrot to talk, you need a larger vocabulary than the parrot." In order to evangelize, the Christian needs to be prepared.

The Christian does not need to be a theological scholar to evangelize. One does not need to have a voice like Billy Graham to speak forth the Truth. Sometimes, Christians use the preparation stage as an excuse to not evangelize. They may share that they are not prepared well enough. Preparation is helpful. Preparation is needful. However, preparation is not an excuse for being disobedient in sharing the great news of Jesus Christ. A five-year-old boy went home to share with his mom what he learned at Vacation Bible School. Each finger represented a verse about salvation. The boy joyfully shared each verse represented by each finger perfectly. By the time he reached the last verse, the mother gave her life to Christ. How could that happen? The five-year-old boy was not a rehearsed evangelist. The little boy shared Truth, and God used the Truth to convert the soul (Romans 10:17). Even children have a part in evangelizing (Mark 10:15).

The Christian has the responsibility to evangelize. The Christian has the responsibility to share what he knows of Truth at all levels of his growth. Notice that the Bible *does* encourage the believer to grow in grace and knowledge of Jesus (2 Peter

3:18). Each believer should aspire to know God more (Psalm 27:4; Philippians 3:8). Each believer must be prepared to give a reason for the hope within them (1 Peter 3:15).

The tenure of Scripture is that the Christian be prepared in mind, attitude, feet, and heart. 1 Peter 3:15 says: *"...always be ready to make a defense to everyone who asks you to give an account for the hope that is in you..."* In order to make a defense or to share about the Christian hope, there needs to be a mind that is prepared.

Remember the commercial: "The mind is a terrible thing to waste"? As Christians we are to *renew* our minds (Romans 12:1-2). Paul prays for the church of Ephesus to have wisdom in the knowledge of Him, and that they be enlightened to know what the hope of His calling is (Ephesians 1:16-18). It is said that when one gets saved, over forty different things happen to him. Grow in understanding of those things. Paul even reasoned with Jews about the Scriptures (Acts 17:2). How? He prepared his mind.

No one should better know the gospel than the Christian. The gospel is the good news of Jesus

Christ. It is *"the power of God unto salvation"* (Romans 1:16). If one needs salvation, there must be some bad news before we can see good news. The reason the unsaved need the gospel is because they are sinners. All have sinned before the holy standard of God (Ecclesiastes 7:20; Psalm 53:2-3; Romans 3:23). There is no way man's "good" works can earn him a right in heaven (Isaiah 64:6; Ephesians 2:8-9; Romans 4). As good as someone may appear to be, they still do not reach heaven's standard, which is perfection (Matthew 5:48).

The point of Scripture is to make it clear that no one is perfect, and that all are lost and destined for hell. This is where the good news comes in. The heart of the gospel can be found in 1 Corinthians 15:1-5. Jesus, the perfect God/man, came to save (John 1:29; Hebrews 4:15; 1 Peter 3:18). Jesus died for sins. Jesus rose again. All of this is according to the Scriptures. The sinner must repent and put his trust completely in the person, power and promise of Christ (Luke 24:46-48; Acts 16:30-31; 20:21; Romans 4:21; 2 Timothy 3:15). Only Jesus can save a sinner! This is the gospel! This is the good news that the sinner needs to know and trust. The Christian needs to be clear about the good news (gospel) that saved the soul.

Christians can prepare their mind with daily readings of the Bible. How are your quiet times with God? Have you read through the Bible? Missionary Wilson knew of a crippled man that dragged himself for days through the African jungle just to hear more of the Word of God. Isn't it great that you do not have to drag your body through mosquito-infested, humid jungles to hear the Word? However, you may have to drag your tired body out of bed earlier. Whatever time you read the Bible, that is fine, but just read it.

Christians are to be involved with their local church (Hebrews 10:25). If you have a New Testament, Bible-believing church, there ought to be proper teaching of the Word. The pastors have the responsibility to equip the saints to a better understanding of their faith (Ephesians 4:11-16). Listen, if your church does not prepare your mind for growth, you need to talk to your leadership about the Ephesians text. Be gracious about it. If your leadership doesn't desire to help you grow in your knowledge of the hope giving by God, it may be time to find another church. Don't waste your mind. Get your mind prepared.

Not only is the mind to be prepared for evangelism, but attitudes need to be prepared. First Peter 3:15 states that we ought to *"give an account with reverence."* Reverence has with it an understanding of respect. Just because an unsaved person does not hold to your Christian worldview, you do not have the grounds to manifest disrespectful attitudes. Romans 12 reminds the Christian within society to be respectful, peaceful, and to overcome evil with good. Titus 3:2 adds to this list that the Christian is to show consideration to every man. Why should we have these types of attitudes? It is a reflection on the Lord we represent. We are to reflect Christ to the world. Jesus told His disciples that they will know them by their Christ-like love (John 13:34-35).

I heard of a famous pastor who witnessed with great reasoning ability when he was still a seminary student. He shared with strong conviction, showing the superiority of the Christian belief. He had rationally shown his unsaved co-worker that he was totally wrong in his belief system, and that he needed Christ. The co-worker retorted, "I agree that you are smarter than me, but I am not going to accept your Christ, for I can't stand you!" Those words cut the young seminary student. It was a good reminder that we are to be prepared in our attitudes when evangelizing.

Compassion should be the Christian attitude. The Christian needs to remember from where they came. We too were sinners, lost on our way to hell (Titus 3:3-5). God saved us according to His kindness. We are to reflect Christ in our attitudes as we evangelize.

We also need to prepare our feet for action. Romans 10:15 reminds the Christian that good news spoken meant that feet brought the messenger. In other words, our feet need to be willing to go to share Christ (Matthew 28:19). I have heard of Christians that "wait for God" to bring the unsaved to their door. They are quick to defend themselves by showing that they did not force any conversation upon those who do not want to listen. However, respect does not mean disobedience to the Lord's command (Mark 16:15; Luke 24:46-48; Romans 1:14-15). Christians need to prepare their feet to go. It is possible to go to the unsaved and direct conversations toward God with all respect and consideration.

A young man was on a beach filled with starfish. The sun was going to dry them out. He started to throw some back into the ocean. A curious observer shouted out, "You'll never get all of them back in time." The young man responded, "But, I just made a difference with this one!", and he threw another into the water to be saved from the sun. In a similar way, we must be motivated for that one soul. Christians who find excuses not to move their feet for evangelism will not make a difference for God's kingdom.

It is interesting that the armor of the Christian has a piece for the feet. The gospel of peace is part of the armor that covers the feet (Ephesians 6:15). When one obeys the Lord in evangelizing, the enemy is resisted. The Christian stands firm by evangelizing. Isn't that true? Don't you find that, when you evangelize, your faith grows stronger? There may be times that the unsaved ask hard questions, but it motivates us to grow in our preparation of knowledge. Obedience to God brings strength to stand.

We need to also be prepared in the heart. We

need to evaluate ourselves and make sure that we are motivated by God's love (2 Corinthians 5:14). First Corinthians 13:1-8 reminds us to do the work of the Lord with love. We need to love God with all our heart. We need to love our neighbor (Luke 10). The good Samaritan was a great rebuke to the religious Jews. They lacked love. May that not be the case of the Christian in evangelization.

Lastly, the Christian needs to prepare their heart for rejection. John 15:18-19 states that the world rejected Christ, so they will reject those who witness about Christ. The heart should be ready for this disappointment. Remember, wide is the way to destruction. It is not that we get callous towards rejection, but we need to remember that our faithfulness is not on the basis of acceptance or rejection of our message. Our faithfulness is based on Christ. Our identity is secure in Christ (Ephesians 1). We are overcomers by Christ alone (1 John 5:4).

Our heart needs to be prepared to be rejected. In 2 Timothy 1:8, Paul reminds Timothy that those who proclaim the gospel may have to suffer for the gospel. The Christian needs to prepare their heart for that reality by God's grace. Our hearts need to be *prepared* for evangelism.

| 3 |

Proclamation

Romans 1:15 "...I am eager to preach the gospel..."

The Christian has the responsibility to *proclaim* Christ. Proclaiming or preaching Jesus is the way to the unsaved becoming saved. No one gets saved without getting the gospel of Jesus (Romans 10:13-15). It may be proclaimed by written word or spoken word. In any case, the primary means of evangelism is the Word of God. The seed needs to get out of the bag if there is to be any potential for growth. Remember, it is God that saves. We just need to get the salvation story out. Faith comes by hearing the Word of Christ (Romans 10:17). The Word of God is living, enduring as imperishable seed (1 Peter 1:23). The Word that brought creation from nothing (Genesis 1) is powerful enough to save lost sinners (Romans 1:16).

Notice that we are not commanded to "do" the gospel. We are commanded to preach/proclaim the gospel. Only Jesus "did" the gospel. Only He could die for sins. Only He could rise up to justify sinners. The gospel is not about you and me. It is about Jesus. We are never told to "do" the gospel. Do Christians live the gospel? Is there gospel-living? Yes, but not in a "doing" of the gospel. We live *because* of the gospel. We live lives that revolve around the truth of the gospel. In doing so, we are told to proclaim the gospel. The gospel will obviously transform the unsaved and will have resultant affects. However, we are to proclaim the good news of Christ!

Some Christians get caught up in methods. They believe that a certain method of sharing the gospel is more compelling than the other. Methods change with time. There has been the Romans

Road, 4 Spiritual Laws, Evangelism Explosion, the Way of the Master, and many more. Are they good methods? If they get the Christian to proclaim Christ, they serve a good purpose. Do not let methodology keep you from encouraging others to proclaim Christ.

An old seminary professor shared that there are two ways of going about proclaiming Christ: there is 1) the confrontational way, and 2) the informative way. Confrontational evangelism is where the Christian realizes that they may not get another chance to share with the individual, so they try to get through the whole redemptive story. Obviously, this is what we always want to do with everyone, but there are times that it is not feasible. Confrontational evangelism attempts to get the person to respond in some way. It is a confrontation. It is letting the unsaved know their true spiritual state, and that there are serious consequences for rejecting the gospel.

One time I was flying within Brazil. Sitting by me was a director of a Federal University reading *The Origin of Species* by Darwin. I asked him if he liked what he was reading. This brought up a conversation about creation and evolutionism. After the director made it clear that he had no desire for Truth, I decided to gently remind him of the serious consequences of rejecting the gospel. I reminded him that he will sit before a holy God who will rightly judge him to a lake of fire for eternity. He could not get away from me, for we were at 34,000 feet in the air. He went back to his book. Confrontational evangelism is not being rude, but it is being bold and clear. It is helping the unsaved come to grasps with the awesome reality of accepting or rejecting the gospel.

There is another way of evangelism that is an informative style. This is where one may only have time to share some truths of the gospel. This may be as little as "Jesus loves you." An evangelist shared the story of church members being convicted to share Jesus. One man knew he should share with his neighbor.

One morning as the neighbors saw each other getting into their cars for work, the Christian felt the need to share something. Scared to death to say anything religious, the Christian ducked into his vehicle and blurted out, "Jesus loves you, neighbor." He then drove away. Another Christian was convicted to share something about God with her family member, so she picked up the phone to call him. After some superficial conversation, she stated, "Jesus loves you," and then hung up. There was yet another member of the church that felt convicted to share Jesus with someone. Feeling convicted while he was getting a haircut, he shared with the barber, "Jesus loves you." The barber swung his chair around, and shouted out, "You are the third person today to share that with me!" This opened for more informative conversation. You never know how God will use a nugget of Truth. Whether it is confrontational or informative evangelism, we must proclaim the Truth.

One of the ways to help the unsaved know more about the Word of God is doing Bible studies with them. Doing Bible studies with the unsaved is great! The book of John was written to help the unsaved believe in Jesus for eternal life (John 20:31).

A simple study in the book of John is an excellent start. If you do not have a study in John to use, seek out a pastor of your local church to help make a study for the unsaved. Listen, many reasons Christians refrain from doing Bible studies with the unsaved is because they have never asked.

Ask an unsaved person if they are willing to do a study about Jesus from the book of John. Remember to prepare your heart for rejection. However, keep up the pursuit of proclaiming Christ through evangelistic Bible studies. What a joy when you find a person that is willing to study God's infinite Word!

I have asked scores of people to study God's Word. When I find an unbeliever willing to study the book of John, it reminds me that God is at work drawing others (John 6:44). I am not alone in the pursuit of sharing Christ. The Holy Spirit works in convicting the unsaved (John 16:8). This brings encouragement in asking others to study the greatest news ever. God is alive and at work! We need to be willing to join in the work of evangelism. We need to be willing to open our mouths and proclaim God's Word.

We need to trust God to work through the gospel. The word of the cross is *"the power of God for those being saved"* (1 Corinthians 1:18). Paul was eager to preach the gospel. Why? It is *"the power of God for salvation"* (Romans 1:16). We don't need to trust gimmicks to convict the unsaved. We don't need to trust friendships to convict the unsaved. We need to trust the gospel of Christ.

One time I was in Italy doing ministry. I was talking to a young missionary who was excited to reach the Italians for the Lord. I asked him what he was doing to reach them. He shared with me how he was developing friendships. He shared how, with building trust over time, he would eventually get to the gospel. He called this friendship evangelism. I gently reminded him that no one gets saved by having friendships. The gospel needs to be proclaimed (1 Corinthians 15:1-5; Romans 10:13-15). I challenged him to give the gospel, and when they reject the message, seek to still be as friendly as possible. We need to trust in God's powerful work through the proclamation of Truth in love.

Christians may share the gospel, and as they proclaim Christ, not see any "results." This can be discouraging. Our culture is one of instant gratification. We are a results-oriented people. We want instant success. Remember, we need to entrust the results to God. It is God that opens hearts (Acts 16:14). It is God that opens minds to Truth (Luke 24:45; Acts 9; 1 Corinthians 2:14). It is God that saves! We cannot save anyone.

Here is an example. John is asked to preach at an evangelistic service. John gives a clear message of the gospel. No one gets saved. The next evangelistic service, Jerry is asked to preach. Jerry preaches a clear message of the gospel. No one gets saved. The next evangelistic service, Ted is asked to come and preach. The church listens to Ted's sermon on the gospel message. Twenty people get saved that day. Who is going to be asked to come back to preach at the church's next evangelistic outreach? Will it be John, Jerry, or Ted? They all preached a clear message of the gospel, but the church will most likely pick Ted! It was Ted's sermon that brought twenty people to Christ! The church may even say that Ted has the gift of evangelism. Why? There were apparent results when he preached! First Corinthians 3:7 reminds the Christian that Ted is nothing in the process, but it is all about God. The results are left in His hand. We need to be faithful witnesses of the gospel. We need to proclaim Him.

Will you be faithful in proclaiming Christ even when there are no apparent results? Remember, the results are to be entrusted to God. An elderly Australian believer never saw results from distributing evangelistic tracks, but he faithfully shared Christ. One day, three evangelists were speaking at a conference. During the time of fellowship, they shared with one another how they came to the Lord. All three were on vacation at different times in Australia. All three had received tracts from the elderly man. They decided to go back and find that man. The elderly man was thrilled to see that God used his form of getting the Word out. In thirty years of passing out tracts and sharing Christ, he had never seen results until those evangelists shared.

God may or may not allow you to see the results on earth, but remember, those who plant and water will receive their reward (1 Corinthians 3:8). Be faithful to trust God with the results!

A quick side note for parents: God is the only one that can save your child. Be careful to not manipulate your child into a false decision for Christ. Be faithful in praying for your child. Be faithful in showing Christ's love. Be faithful in showing Christ's Lordship in the home. Be faithful to proclaim Christ. But, don't make your child "saved" by your wit and zeal. Let God work. Let it be genuine. Trust Him with the results!

| 4 |

Purpose

Mark 1:17 "...Follow Me, and I will make you become fishers of men."

The Christian's responsibility in evangelism is to be *purposeful*. The Christian ought to be intentional to share the good news of Jesus. I know of a believer that intentionally prays for the unsaved by name daily. He intentionally calls them each week with the purpose of sharing about what he prays for them. His purposeful living of evangelism has given him many opportunities to see others come to Christ. Colossians 4:5 states: *"Conduct yourselves with wisdom toward outsiders, making the most of the opportunity."* The believer ought to conduct their life in such a way to evangelize others.

Think about Sunday mornings. Don't you wake up with the purpose of going to church to worship the Lord? You may even have another day where your purpose is to meet with other believers to edify one another. But, do you have a day purposed for evangelism? The purposes of the Christian are to exalt God, edify the saints, and evangelize the lost. The whole week is to exemplify those purposes. However, you may select specific times of the week so that you purposefully proclaim Christ to a neighbor, or a family member. You may set up a lunch date with a co-worker with the intention of sharing the good news of how Jesus transformed your life.

The Great Commission mandates believers to make disciples from all nations (Matthew 28:18-20). Jesus told His disciples that if they followed Him that they would become fishers of men (Mark 1:17). If Christians imitate Christ, they will fish for men. This is purposeful living.

Take a moment to evaluate your week. Do you find that you are living wisely? Are you seeking to live in such a way that values time to witness for Christ? Do you see your daily contacts as potential lives to be saved by Christ? Are you seeking ways to get to know your neighbor? Have you asked your pastoral staff about ways that you can help with outreach ministries? Are you praying for the lost? Are you seeking to offer them evangelistic Bible studies?

Acts 1:8 reminds the Christian that they are to be witnesses of Christ in different spheres of influence. The disciples started in Jerusalem. It was not their hometown, but it was a familiar place. It was a hostile place, but the place designated by our Lord. The Lord saved many Jews and the church grew. The church grew into Samaria where the Samaritans heard the good news of Christ (Acts 8). Then, the Gentiles were reached in Acts 10-11. God in His sovereign plan has people to be reached with the gospel.

This includes you. God has sovereignly permitted you to have the influences that you have. Think about your life! You are here because of God! You got saved because of God! You have a special sphere of contacts because of God! Where you live, where you shop, where you work, where you eat or play…it is all permitted by God's grace. Your pastor does not have your job. Your pastor does not have your family. Your pastor does not have your sphere of influence. God wants you to be a light to those whom He sovereignly allowed in your life. Seek to share Christ with those under your sphere of influence.

Paul knew that his purpose in life was to share Christ to kings, Jews and Gentiles (Acts 9:15; 26:16-18). He took his freedom in Christ, and limited it to love Jews and Gentiles (1 Corinthians 9:19-20), seeing people in light of the gospel. Paul saw himself as a key instrument in getting the gospel out so that others may be saved (1 Corinthians 9:22; 10:33). Paul said: *"Woe is me if I do not preach the gospel"* (1 Corinthians 9:16). Paul knew that he had to be a part of the greatest program on earth—proclaiming Christ. He disciplined himself to not be disqualified (1 Corinthians 9:27-10:13). How is your discipline? Are you using your freedoms in Christ to win souls (1 Corinthians 9:22)? Beware that you do not get distracted with worldliness, but stay focused on one of God's purposes for your life—evangelism.

| 5 |

Perception

Acts 17:22-23 "…Paul stood…and said, 'Men of Athens, I observe that you are very religious…what you worship in ignorance, this I proclaim to you.'"

The Christian responsibility in evangelism is to be *perceptive*. Perceptiveness has more to do than just being able to see clearly. It has the idea of understanding what is being seen. It is interpreting your situation wisely.

The world is our mission field, and the Scriptures give a clear image of the spiritual state of mankind. The Christian needs to have a biblical understanding of the lost. Everyone that does not know the Lord is lost in their sins, heading to hell.

Rob was looking around at the things being sold at a neighborhood garage sale. The owner of the garage sale had a "Bound to Hell" tattoo that was visible. Rob inquired about the tattoo. The man responded, "Oh, it was something I did while in the service." Rob continued in witnessing to the man. Rob asked, "So, what do you think? Are you going to hell when you die?" The man thought about his life and concluded, "Yeah, I am going to hell." Rob quickly interjected, "No, you are not going to hell, but you are going to hell forever!" The lost are in an eternal condemnation (Matthew 25:46). There is a great need for the salvation message to be shared.

The Christian needs to perceive that the lost are dead in their sins spiritually. When Adam and Eve sinned, they fled the presence of God (Genesis 3:8). Sin separated man from God (Isaiah 59:2). Death is a separation (James 2:26), and the wages of sin is death (Romans 6:23). Man's spiritual state is a separation from God (Ephesians 2:1). All men are under the control and condemnation of sin (Romans 3:8-9).

Not only is man dead to God, but he is blinded by Satan (2 Corinthians 4:4). Satan holds the unsaved within his domain (1 John 5:19; Ephesians 2:2; Acts 26:18). Jesus said that Satan even takes the Word out of man's heart, so that he may not get saved (Luke 8:12).

I do not know how many times that I have seen the lost get distracted during a gospel appeal. There are times when the phone rings, and just "happens" to ring at a critical moment in the presentation. There are times when a child screams bloody murder to draw the parent away from the gospel appeal. There are many schemes used by Satan to take away the Word of salvation. Christian, don't forget that you are in a spiritual battle. The enemy is real. You are invading his territory. Pray, prepare, perceive, and proclaim!

The lostness of the unsaved ought to encourage the believer in evangelism. How? There is no gimmick or manipulation that can bring life to the unsaved. What man can bring about life spiritually? The power of eternal life is not in your cleverness of speech, but it is in the gospel. The

Christian needs to make the gospel clear. They do not need to use persuasive words or flattering words (1 Corinthians 1:17; 2:4). They must trust the Word. They must remember that the unsaved need the Truths of God's infinite powerful Word.

Understanding that the unsaved are lost ought to help the Christian's expectation in evangelism. I don't expect the unsaved to agree with a biblical worldview. I don't expect the unsaved to act like a regenerate Christian. I don't expect their thoughts, vocabulary, political views, and actions line up with Scripture. Why? They are lost! There is no reason to argue with the unsaved or get bent-out-of-shape with them. They are dead and blinded. They need to see God's love and God's Truths.

Perceptiveness is to understand the culture of your hearer. What do you assume when you tell someone: "If you were to die today, why would God allow you to enter heaven?" There is the presumption that the evangelized believes in heaven, God, or even death. I once saw a report on a group that believed that they would not die. What denial! The Christian needs to perceive the background of the hearer.

The Christian also needs to understand the influence of the culture behind the hearer. Why? So that proper communication can be done. Jesus was the master communicator. He knew the culture of His hearer. He knew that they would understand the lilies of the field imagery (Matthew 6:28) or sheep parallels (John 10).

Paul perceived the culture behind his audience and knew the importance of communicating clearly. The book of Acts recounts some of Paul's discernment in understanding his audience. When Paul witnessed to Jews, he quoted the Old Testament. Why? The Jews had a respect for the Hebrew Scriptures. Paul would reason from the Old Testament about the Christ (Acts 17:2), and the Jews understood Old Testament references. Paul knew that they were familiar with such Truths. This was why Paul reasoned with them from the Scriptures.

When Paul arrived at Athens, he perceived the Greeks' background (Acts 17:18, 23). When Paul was before the Areopagus, he began with their understanding of religion (Acts 17:22). Instead of quoting Old Testament Scripture, he started with God as Creator of all in the world (Acts 17:24). He even cited one of their prophets as it related to truth (Acts 17:28). Though Paul's approach started differently than with the Jews, he made sure to get to Jesus and the gospel (Acts 17:31). Paul sought to understand the culture of his hearers in order to communicate clearly to them. He disciplined himself to live in such a way to win his audience for Christ (1 Corinthians 9:19).

I was on a flight from Chicago to Kansas City. There were very few people on this flight. I noticed a Catholic priest sitting by himself, so I decided to talk to him. I asked him, "According to your religion, what does one have to do in order to be saved?" He responded, "One must receive Jesus as Lord and Savior." If I had no understanding of his culture, I could have walked away thinking the priest was like a protestant. However, I suspected that he had a different definition for "receive" as well as his concept of Jesus. After talking to him for a while, he admitted that he believed the Bible was full of errors since it did not support his religious views. It was important to know a little of his potential background, and it was important to verify that through a frank conversation.

Perception is important. If a Christian is to witness effectively, they will seek to understand their hearer. It is important to remember that the lost are dead in their sins and blinded by Satan. It is important to discern the hearer's definitions of vocabulary. It is important to understand their background in order to communicate clearly. The Christian has the responsibility of being perceptive in evangelism.

| 6 |

Provision

Philippians 4:18 "But I have received everything in full and have an abundance; I am amply supplied, having received from Epaphroditus what you have sent, a fragrant aroma, an acceptable sacrifice, well-pleasing to God."

The Christian has the responsibility of *provision* for evangelism. Provision is not in the sense of making time for evangelism, although we have covered that importance previously. Provision is in the sense of physical help. It is monetary related, and yet more than just money. It could be hospitality, or the help of transportation for evangelism.

Paul encouraged the church of Philippi as it gave finances to help the gospel ministry (Philippians 4:15-19). Paul reminded the church that their giving was *"well-pleasing to God"* (Philippians 4:18). The church of Antioch sent out Barnabas and Paul (Acts 13:3). They sailed to Cyprus, which means that they purchased passages. The implication is that the church helped them in this mission. Paul exhorts Titus to provide transportation for Zenas and Apollos through the good efforts of the believers on the Island of Crete (Titus 3:13-14). Scripture encourages the believer to provide for gospel ministry.

I remember an outreach ministry being proposed by a certain pastor. The pastor shared the purpose of evangelism. He shared how this ministry is a great opportunity to reach people in the given community. However, the pastor shared there was one problem. There were no budgeted finances for this ministry. After the pastor shared, an elderly couple approached him and gave $10,000 to the cause. They had been waiting to give towards something related to evangelism. That couple gave a shot of encouragement to that outreach ministry!

Where a man's treasurer is, so is his heart (Matthew 6:21). The Christian should have a heart for missions. The Christian should have a heart for providing the finances needed to do the work of evangelism.

How are you doing in your giving towards evangelism? Do you invest in buying Bibles for the unsaved? Do you invest in taking an unsaved person out to eat to share the gospel? Are you first to volunteer to loan your car for transportation related to missions and evangelism? Are you excited to house a missionary? Do you seek out your pastoral leadership, asking how you can provide finances for an outreach ministry? This a brief chapter, but the point is simple and clear: God provides for evangelism through His people. Is He using you?

| 7 |

Praise

Revelation 5:12 "…worthy is the Lamb that was slain to receive power and riches and wisdom and might and honor and glory and blessing."

The Christian has the responsibility in evangelism to *praise* God. All things are to be done for the glory of God (Romans 11:36; 1 Corinthians 10:31). In the context of evangelism, the Great Commission was never given to man for man to be praised. It was given so that the Lord would be praised.

The church at Corinth wanted to praise the men who evangelized. Some praised Paul while others praised Apollos (1 Corinthians 3:4). The apostle Paul reminded the church that neither men are to be the focus: *"So neither he who plants nor he who waters is anything, but only God who gives the growth"* (1 Corinthians 3:7).

Sometimes we can be egocentric. We focus on ourselves. It is where we give excuses for not sharing the good news of Jesus. A Christian may say: "I don't speak well" or "I can't share the Bible like so and so." These are phrases that reflect giving praise to man. When Moses tried these excuses, God rebuked him and reminded him that it was He who made the tongue (Exodus 4:10-11). Paul wanted God to be glorified, and he knew that his words just needed to reflect to others the power of the gospel (1 Corinthians 2:1-5).

Even the lifestyle of the evangelist is to praise God. Your good behavior is not to lift up your praise, but the praise of your God. Matthew 5:16 reminds the believer to let his light shine before men, so that glory is given to our heavenly Father. The unsaved ought to see a difference in Christians lives, not to bring glory to the Christian, but glory to God who transformed the Christian. All praise to God!

When Peter shared the report of how God had saved the Gentile Cornelius just as He saved Jews, the leadership of the Jerusalem church glorified God (Acts 11:18). Paul and Barnabas gathered the Antioch church that had sent them on their missionary journey. They shared with the church how God had opened a door of faith to the Gentiles (Acts 14:27). There ought to be worship services reflecting on God's salvation reaching to the nations (Psalm 96). God deserves the praise!

Evangelism is to the praise of our Lord. Results of evangelism are to the praise of our God. Without the Triune God working in evangelism, nothing can be accomplished. The church ought to gather to share what God is doing in evangelism and missions. There needs to be praise about God using our words and works. There ought to be praise given to our Lord individually and corporately for what God is doing through us in evangelism.

| 8 |

Conclusion

1 Corinthians 9:17 "...I have a stewardship entrusted to me."

For the Christians, there are many responsibilities. They are privileges that we ought to do with the motive of love towards our great God. Evangelism is about being obedient. Evangelism is an act of faith. Evangelism is God's process of getting the good news of Jesus Christ out to a lost world. Evangelism is the responsibility of the Christian.

Let us be encouraged to know that God is

building His Church (Matthew 16:18). The Church can only truly grow with transformed lives (1 Corinthians 1:2), and those lives are transformed by the power of the gospel. How do they get the gospel? The gospel is communicated via the Christian.

Do not give up sharing the good news of Jesus! Maybe you have shared with many people and have not seen any fruit for your labor. Remain faithful! The God who converted all of Nineveh can still convert your whole city (Matthew 12:41). Dr. Jordan was asked by a church member when he would be satisfied with the size of his church. His response was: "When we put a roof over the whole city!" The church needs to continue evangelizing.

One of the most memorable funerals that I have ever attended was of an elderly man in my home church. Mr. G. had a reputation of sharing his faith. He found joy in sharing Jesus. At his funeral, someone read a letter he wrote before passing away. It started like this: "This will be the last time I evangelize you..." I was in tears! It was great! Mr. G. was thoughtful of the lost person without a Bible at his own funeral, so he had planned for men to give out Bibles to those who did not have one. What a testimony! What an encouragement for evangelism!

It is important to remember Christ's attitude about evangelism. Some religious people grumbled about Christ's work of evangelism, so He told three parables. He told the parable of the lost sheep, lost coin, and the prodigal son (Luke 15). All three parables have the same people represented: Jesus, the Pharisees, and the sinners. Jesus is represented as the shepherd, woman, and the father. The Pharisees are represented by the ninety-nine sheep, nine silver coins, and the older son. The sinner is represented by the lost sheep, lost silver coin, and the lost son.

Jesus' point was to show that there should be rejoicing over the lost being brought back to fellowship. The unsaved that repent bring great joy to heaven (Luke 15:7), and it should be for the church as well. If you are one to grumble about evangelism, ask yourself if you are being like the Pharisees. The Pharisees needed to repent (Luke 15:7 with 16:15). Are you truly saved? Do you have joy in sharing Christ?

There is much more that can be said about

evangelism. More can be shared about our responsibility of prayer, preparation, proclamation, purpose, perception, provision, and praise in relation to evangelism. As we follow Christ, may we grow in the grace and knowledge of Him to be Christlike fishers of men.

www.ingramcontent.com/pod-product-compliance
Lightning Source LLC
Chambersburg PA
CBHW072209100526
44589CB00015B/2444